I0004629

Raspberry Pi

A Beginner's Guide To The Raspberry Pi

Sydney Johnson

PUBLISHED BY:

Sydney Johnson

Disclaimer

The information contained in this book is for general information purposes only. The information is provided by the authors and while we endeavor to keep the information up to date and correct, we make no representations or warranties of any kind, express or implied, about the completeness, accuracy, reliability, suitability or availability with respect to the book or the information, products, services, or related graphics contained in the book for any purpose. Any reliance you place on such information is therefore strictly at your own risk.

Table of Contents

Chapter 1: Introduction

Welcome to this entry-level guide to the Raspberry Pi! In this guide we will be introducing you to the Raspberry Pi device and its basic features, functions and capabilities.

In section one of this guide we will be discussing the following aspects of the Raspberry Pi:

- ➢ What the Raspberry Pi is
- ➢ The history of the Raspberry Pi
- ➢ The relationship between the Raspberry Pi and programming

Please note that this guide refers exclusively to the Raspberry Pi Model B. The Model A, while being cheaper, comes with no ethernet port, half the USB ports and half the memory. The model A is meant for very specific project which don't need the Raspberry Pi to act as a full computer. For example as a control system for home automation. Therefore, for beginner users, we do not recommend purchasing the model A.

All references to operating system commands refer to Raspbian, a special version of Debian Linux which is the operating system we recommend for first-time users.

So, let's get started!

1.1What is the Raspberry Pi?

As you probably know, the Raspberry Pi isn't a delicious dessert, but rather an incredible little electronic device that has revolutionised computer science education and re-imagined what is possible with a low-cost computing device.

That's right, the Raspberry Pi (pictured here) is a fully functional computer that has all the basic features of other personal computers such as laptops, but is much less expensive at 35 American Dollars for the best model.

Even though the Raspberry Pi is only about as large as a credit card, it can be used for computing tasks such as browsing the Web, word processing and watching High Definition (HD) video. It can even be used to play a few basic video games!

Illustration : By Jwrodgers (Own work) [CC-BY-SA-3.0

The Raspberry Pi is also very power efficient and can be powered by most USB power sources. For example, the charger that powers your smartphone is a good source of power for your Raspberry Pi as long as it conforms to the safe voltage standards for USB devices.

By using a voltage regulator it is even possible to power a Raspberry Pi with AA batteries, opening up all sorts of applications for the device. Although we do not recommend this for novice users as it may damage the device if done incorrectly.

The Raspberry Pi is of course different in some ways from the computers that you may already know. For one thing, the components from which the Raspberry Pi is constructed come from smartphone technology, which is one of the reasons it is so power efficient.

One of the most important components of the Raspberry Pi is its CPU or Central Processing Unit. This is the "brain" of the computer and this is where the largest difference between computers made by Intel Corporation or AMD and the Raspberry Pi reveals itself.

The Raspberry Pi (and most modern tablet computers and smart phones) have a different "architecture" than traditional computers. We won't go into exactly what this means, just know that the two types of computers speak very different "languages" and therefore programs written for one CPU will not be understood by another. Incidentally, the names of the architectures are "x86" in the case of traditional computers and "ARM" in the case of the Raspberry Pi.

Let's have a quick look at the technical specifications of the Raspberry Pi, don't worry if you don't understand exactly what these terms mean. We'll be explaining them shortly. Please note that these are the specifications for the Model "B" Raspberry Pi, which is the better specified version of the computer:

- 700 MHz ARM1176JZF-S core
- Broadcom VideoCore IV
- 512 MB (shared with GPU) 2 (via integrated USB hub)
- Composite RCA (PAL and NTSC), HDMI (rev 1.3 & 1.4),raw LCD Panels via DSI.HDMI resolutions from 640×350 to 1920×1200 plus various PAL and NTSC standards.
- 3.5 mm jack, HDMI for audio
- SD / MMC / SDIO card slot

➤ 10/100 Ethernet (RJ45)

The first listing refers to the aforementioned ARM CPU of the computer. "700 Mhz" is a measurement of the speed or frequency at which the CPU operates. A higher number usually means better performance, but this comparison is only straightforward when comparing CPUs that are otherwise similar.

The Broadcom VideoCore IV is the processor that handles the video and graphical functions of the computer. The Raspberry Pi can handle full High Definition video and has 3D graphics power comparable to the first Xbox video game console.

The Raspberry Pi has 512 Megabytes of RAM (Random Access Memory), which is the "working memory" of the computer. Data that is waiting to be processed or is coming from the CPU resides here. With the Pi this memory is shared between the CPU and graphics processor.

You will also notice that the Raspberry Pi has two display connectors; one is an HDMI port for High Definition display devices such as plasma or LCD flatscreen televisions and the other is a composite RCA connector suitable to connect to most Standard Definition televisions. You should always choose to connect through HDMI if possible, since the picture quality and resolution is far better and will provide a more pleasant user experience.

If you should need to use the RCA connector then you will also need the 3.5 mm audio jack for sound, in the case of HDMI both sound and video are carried by the same cable.

The Raspberry Pi doesn't have a hard disk drive with moving mechanical parts in the way that most notebook and desktop computers do. Instead, it uses *solid state digital* (SD) cards

1.2 The History of the Raspberry Pi

The Raspberry Pi was first conceived of at the Computer Lab of the University of Cambridge by four lecturers. Alan Mycroft, Jack Lang, Rob Mullins and Eben Mullins were becoming concerned by the lack of basic programming skills apparent in the new students that were enrolling for Computer Science. In the 90s most of the students coming into Computer Science studies were already equipped with good programming skills. This was most likely due to the fact that computer enthusiasts during that time period needed such skills to get the most from their computers. As the 20th century ended computers became ever more sophisticated and user friendly. Therefore it was not necessary to have such good programming skills just to make use of a computer.

Add to that parents were not likely to let their children tinker with and reprogram expensive devices and modern consumer computing devices such as smartphones, tablets and notebooks and stands to reason that newly enrolled Computer Science students were coming into higher education less and less well equipped.

It was from this need, identified in 2006, that the Raspberry Pi project was conceived. An inexpensive, robust and easy to hack device which would allow a new generation of students that were not afraid to engage with the core technologies involved in computing.

1.3 What's the connection between the Raspberry Pi and Programming?

As you may have been able to tell from section 1.2, one of the main reasons the Raspberry Pi was developed came from the need for a low-cost, easy to maintain computer that represents a safe environment in which to learn computer programming. That's exactly what you Raspberry Pi is best at. The special lightweight operating system Raspbian (Which we'll discuss later) comes as standard with the Python programming environment, in fact that's there the "Pi" in Raspberry Pi comes from![1] There are however many other programming languages that have been ported to the Pi, including (but not limited to):

➤ HTML5
➤ Java
➤ Javascript

---

[1]   http://www.dummies.com/how-to/content/top-ten-programming-languages-ported-to-the-raspbe.html

- ➢ C++
- ➢ C
- ➢ Perl

If you want a computer on which you can learn to program and experiment without having to worry about expensive mistakes, the Raspberry Pi provides just such a solution. After all, that's what it was designed for.

Chapter 2: Essential Accessories for the Raspberry Pi

The Raspberry Pi by itself is great, but it won't do much without a few essential accessories. These are not the only accessories for the Raspberry Pi, but they are needed to operate the computer.

2.1 The Power Source

Illustration: By Smial (Own work) [FAL or GFDL 1.2 (http://www.gnu.org/licenses/old-licenses/fdl-1.2.html)], via Wikimedia Commons

The Raspberry Pi uses a 5 Volt micro-USB power source. Although any micro-USB power source will power the computer, it needs to have sufficient current to provide for stable operations. Every peripheral you connect to the Raspberry Pi adds to the total power requirements, so keep that in mind when selecting a power source.

The creators of the computer recommend using a 5v 1.2A (1200mA) power supply for a decent safety margin, but the device actually needs between 700-1000 mA for the model B board.[2]

Because connecting peripherals such as some keyboards and mouse or a USB Wi-Fi dongle can draw more than the 1 Ampere design specification of the Raspberry Pi, it is recommended that you check the power requirements of each peripheral. If you need more power than can be drawn from the computer, consider using a powered USB hub in addition to the Raspberry Pi.

2.2 HDMI/DVI/RCA Cables

In order to connect the Raspberry Pi to a display device such as a television you will need the correct connecting cable. For High Definition (HD) and HD Ready televisions it is recommended that you use an HDMI cable. There are no special requirements and any HDMI cable should work.

If you have a display device with DVI rather than HDMI connectivity then you can use an HDMI to DVI converter as pictured here:

---

http://www.raspberrypi.org/faqs

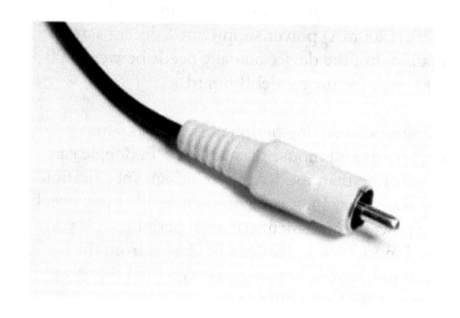

For televisions that lack HDMI you will have to use a RCA cable. You will only need one cable as the audio output using this display method is delivered via a 3.5 mm stereo jack.

2.3 The SD Card

Since the Raspberry Pi does not come with built-in storage, it requires a Solid state Digital (SD) card to store the operating system, programs and data files necessary for its operation. It is recommended that at least a 4Gb Class 4 unit is used for full use of your computer. Logically, the larger the card the less you need to worry. Get the largest and fastest card you can afford. Some SD cards have compatibility problems with the Raspberry Pi and you may want to consider buying a branded Raspberry Pi card that comes pre-loaded with an operating system. elinux.com keeps a list of tested SD cards for the Raspberry Pi at http://elinux.org/RPi_SD_cards, do a little bit of research on the card you intend to get and its compatibility with the Raspberry Pi.

2.4 USB Hub

As mentioned above, the power envelope of the Raspberry Pi is rather modest, so if you intend to hook up power-hungry devices we recommend that you use a powered hub. This is also a must if you need more devices connected than the two built-in USB ports can accommodate.

Illustration: CC Attribution Licence Simon Monk
http://learn.adafruit.com/assets/113 78

2.5 Keyboard and Mouse

The Raspberry Pi doesn't have PS/2 ports, so keyboards and mouse need to use USB in order to connect to the computer. It is a good strategy to use a wireless keyboard and mouse set that shares a single USB receiver, leaving one port free for a Wi-Fi USB device, as an example. Since the keyboard and mouse would then be battery powered you only need to be mindful of the receiver's power draw. Be sure to check whether the particular keyboard and mouse combination you are considering is compatible with the Raspberry Pi online. See if anyone else has had success with that specific keyboard and mouse. Alternatively, look for recommended models and try to find one that appeals to you.

2.6 Ethernet Cable

The Raspberry Pi comes as standard with a 10/100 RJ45 Ethernet port. There isn't much to say about the port, just connect the Raspberry Pi to your router, hub or other network device using a standard RJ45 Ethernet cable.

*Illustration: By Devcore (Own work) [CC0],
via Wikimedia Commons*

2.7 USB Wi-Fi

If Ethernet is not convenient then you can use a USB
Wi-Fi device, please search the Internet to see if the
device you want to use is compatible with the
Raspberry Pi on a hardware level, check that its
power draw is within tolerance and make sure the
operating system you're running works with that
particular Wi-Fi device.

Chapter 3: Connecting Devices to the Raspberry Pi

Now that we have covered the accessories you need to use your Raspberry Pi we'll now look at how everything hooks up.

3.1 Connecting a Display

Connecting a display to your Raspberry Pi is very simple, if your display supports HDMI then simply connect the HDMI cable to the HDMI ports on both the Raspberry Pi and the display device. The connectors can only be inserted one way and it doesn't matter which end of the cable is plugged into which device.

You have to use an RCA cable then connect the one end of the cable to the yellow RCA jack on the computer and the other to the "video in" port on the display device.

3.2 Connecting Audio

If you are using HDMI then it is not necessary to connect additional audio cabling, as the HDMI port also carries audio data.

If you are using an RCA connection or if your HDMI display doesn't have audio capabilities then you will need to use the 3.5 mm stereo jack on the Raspberry Pi. If you want to use the audio connection on your SDTV and it only supports RCA audio (the red and white RCA connectors) you can purchase an inexpensive stereo-to-RCA converter from most Audio-Visual retailers. Alternatively you can directly use desktop computer speakers.

3.3 Connecting your Keyboard and Mouse

Connect the keyboard and mouse to the Raspberry Pi as you would on any other computer. Simply plug the USB cable of the mouse and/keyboard into the USB ports on the computer. The plugs can only go in one way, so check that you have the head of the cable in the correct orientation before attempting the connection and never force the plug in.

3.4 Connecting to the Network

To connect to the network, simply use a RJ45 Ethernet cable or a USB Wi-Fi "dongle" in the Ethernet and USB ports respectively.

If your router is set to use DHCP to dynamically assign IP addresses then you should not need to do anything further to access the network and internet from your Raspberry Pi.

In order to connect to a Wi-Fi network, use the Wi-Fi configuration tool. Look for this icon on the Desktop:

WiFi Config

This will open a window labelled "wpa_gui".

Click the "scan" button. Another window will open with the scan results. Select your Wi-Fi network's SSID by double-clicking it. Now simply enter the password and connect. You should now be connected to your Wi-Fi LAN.

3.5 Connecting External Storage

Connect external storage via USB, this would include flash memory drives and external hard disks. We recommend that you use a powered USB for external storage that requires more power than the Raspberry Pi can provide.

If you are using the X-environment, which is the graphical interface that "looks like windows", USB storage devices will automatically be made accessible through a process called auto-mounting.

3.6 Connecting Power

To power up the Raspberry Pi, simply plug the USB power source into the micro-USB port. There is no on-off switch on the computer itself, so you need to unplug the power source in order to power off the device. Remember to shut down the Raspberry Pi before disconnecting the power in order to avoid possible corruption of the SD card.

Chapter 4: Operating Systems for Your Raspberry Pi

We've mentioned the operating system a few times above, but in this section we'll look at the core software that drives your Raspberry Pi

4.1 Linux: What is it?

Linux is an operating system designed by Linus Torvalds. It is a Unix-alike operating systems, which is to say that it isn't directly a version of the Unix operating system, but operates in a very similar way. Although you may not use Linux directly in your day-to-day computing tasks, Linux and other Unix derived operating systems are everywhere to be found. The MacOS operating system on Apple computers can trace its heritage back to Unix. The Android smart phone operating system is closely based on the Linux kernel in newer versions and most of the websites you interact with everyday are most likely hosted on a Linux-based server. Linux is powerful, highly customisable and very reliable. Which is why it is chosen for so many serious and mission-critical applications. It has however developed a reputation for being very technical and user unfriendly. This has changed significantly with the advent of user-oriented versions of Linux such as Debian and Ubuntu.

Another important thing to note about Linux is that it is *Open Source Software*. This means that you are free to copy, modify and distribute the software without committing software piracy. It is also one of the reasons the Raspberry Pi is so cost-effective; there is no software cost included in the price.

4.2 Raspbian

Raspbian is a Raspberry Pi optimised version of Debian Linux. Debian Linux is a very popular version or "distribution" of Linux which is very user-friendly. It is so popular that many other Linux distributions are based on Debian, including the well-known Ubuntu and Mint OSes.

While there is a version of Debian that will run on the Raspberry Pi, it is a general system for a wide range of ARM processor powered devices. As such it doesn't take advantage of some of the performance enhancing features contained in the Raspberry Pi hardware. The only reason you would choose vanilla Debian over Raspbian is if the application for your Raspberry Pi required it for technical reasons. Since this is a beginner's guide to the Raspberry Pi we strongly recommend starting with Raspbian until you are well acquainted with the system.

When it comes to the way the operating system works from a user-perspective, Raspbian and Debian are almost indistinguishable. As such you can use Debian help documentation in almost all cases. Instructions that apply to Debian also generally apply to Raspbian.

4.3 Getting Started

Unless you have purchased a pre-loaded Raspbian SD card, your Raspberry Pi will not work out of the box. In order to get and prepare the software necessary to drive your Raspberry Pi, you will need another computer with an SD card reader and a working Internet connection. Many notebook and laptop computers now have SD card readers built-in and you can use an inexpensive USB SD card reader to work with an SD card on a desktop computer. You will also need to download about 1.1 Gb of data, so please make the appropriate arrangements.

4.3.1 Getting the Software you need

Thankfully it is now very simple to get a Raspberry Pi up and running thanks to a software package known as NOOBS. NOOBS is an acronym for New Out Of the Box Software and is a simple way to install an operating system on your Raspberry Pi and also allows for a simple recovery option should something go wrong.

Before we get to NOOBS we first need to prepare the SD card.

4.3.2 Preparing the SD card for NOOBS

First, insert a SD card into your other computer. The card needs to be at least 4Gb in size or larger. Once the SD card is inserted you will have to format it so that the Raspberry Pi can read it.

We are assuming that your other computer is a Windows PC. Download the SD Card Association's formatting tool from https://www.sdcard.org/downloads/formatter_4/eula_windows/

After downloading, install the software and run it. Under "options" set the option labelled "Format Size Adjustment" to "ON".

Make sure the selected SD card is the correct one or you'll lose data!

When you are sure, click the "Format" button and wait for the format of the card to complete.

4.3.3 Downloading NOOBS
Now we have to get the NOOBS system, in your Web browser, go to:

downloads.raspberrypi.org/noobs

Save the file and unzip it somewhere. In Windows this can be done by right-clicking on the zipped file and choosing "Extract all".

Copy the extracted files onto the freshly formatted SD card.

You are now ready to run NOOBS on the Raspberry Pi. Remove the SD card from the other computer, insert it into the Raspberry Pi and connect the power.

4.3.4 Running NOOBS for the first time.
The Raspberry Pi should now boot into the NOOBS environment. If you aren't seeing anything on your display device please refer to 5.3 in order to troubleshoot the issue.

If everything has gone well, you should see the following:

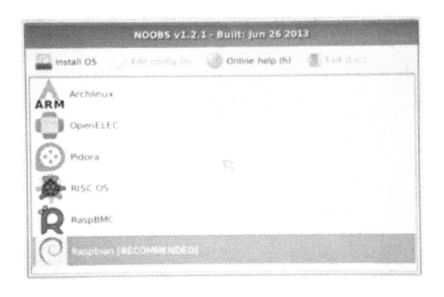

Illustration: CC Attribution Licence Simon Monk
http://learn.adafruit.com/assets/11384

Select Raspbian for now and click on "Install OS", you don't need to be online for this, NOOBS is entirely self contained. Once you've done this you should see the following:

Illustration: CC Attribution Licence Simon Monk
http://learn.adafruit.com/assets/11382

4.3.5 The Raspi-Config Utility
After the installation is complete your Raspberry Pi Should boot into the Raspi-Config utility.

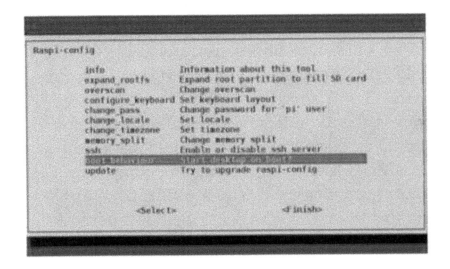

Illustration: Creative Commons Attribution
Simon Monk
http://learn.adafruit.com/assets/11383

The Raspi-config utility is an easy way to change the basic configuration of your Raspberry Pi. Since this is an entry-level guide to the Raspberry Pi we'll only discuss the most important options.

The **"expand_rootfs"** command is used when the root partition, the one upon which the Operating System resides, does not fill up all available space on the SD card. If you used NOOBs to install Raspbian then this should already be done. It may however happen in the future that you wish to upgrade to a larger SD card. In this case you would use a utility such as Win32DiskImager to make a copy of your SD card as an image file. You can then write this image to a larger SD card using the same utility. At this point run Raspi-config again and use the "expand_rootfs" option to utilise the larger card. We'll discuss how to access Raspi-config after the first boot further below.

The **"overscan"** option allows you to set the borders of the display so that the edges of the picture are not cut off.

"configure_keyboard" lets you specify which keyboard layout you are using.

"change pass" lets you change the default password for the Raspberry Pi.

The **locale** and **timezone** setting let you set where you are in the world and what time it is.

"memory_split" lets you adjust how much of the 512Mb RAM goes to the graphics system and how much goes to program memory. Use this only if you know why it needs to be changed. Generally if you need to run applications that are more graphically intensive you may need to shift this number. Follow the guidelines given for individual programs

"boot_behaviour" lets you set the Raspberry Pi to boot straight into the graphical user interface instead of starting at the terminal. It is up to you which option you prefer. The main difference is that you will have to manually start the graphical interface with the command "startx".

4.3.6 Logging in to Raspbian, Creating New Users and Changing Passwords

The default user name for Raspbian is "pi" and the default password is "raspberry". This user account comes preconfigured in Raspbian and is the Admin or "superuser" account.

You don't really want to use the superuser account as your day-to-day account. Therefore we recommend that you also create a normal user account. To do this, either open LX Terminal from the Raspbian Desktop or enter the commands below before issuing "startx". In either case enter the following:

sudo adduser username

Where "username" is the name you choose. After executing this command (by hitting enter) you will be asked for a password and some personal details. Do enter a password, but the rest of the information is optional.

You should now be able to restart the Raspberry Pi and log in with your new user account. Certain actions will require superuser permissions, at this time you can use the superuser credentials to perform those tasks.

You may also wish to change the default password for the superuser account, use Raspi-config or open LXterminal and type:

passwd

You will then be asked for the current password and the new password.

AN IMPORTANT NOTE ABOUT NOOBS:
NOOBS remains on your SD card even after installing an OS. You can run NOOBS by holding "SHIFT" at startup. From here you can recover or install a different operating system.

4.3.7 Installing and Removing Software

For beginners, the simplest way to install software is by using the Raspberry Pi App store. There should be an appropriate icon on the Raspbian Desktop, but if not you simply have to install the store. Open LXterminal and type:

sudo apt-get update && sudo apt-get install pistore

After installation simply double-click the App store Icon and browse the store to find, buy and install software. Please note that an Internet connection is required to make use of the store or install software on the Raspberry Pi.

Chapter 5: Troubleshooting

Sometimes things go wrong. In this section you'll find a short list of common problems and a few tips to help resolve them. There is however a very large and very enthusiastic community on the Web that can help you resolve almost any problem. If you can't find a solution to your problem below then do search for a solution online. The chances are very good that someone else has already solved the issue for you.

5.1 Power Problems

If your Raspberry Pi is not powering up there are a number of things you can try:

> Disconnect all peripherals that are not needed for a power-on test, at a minimum just leave the display and power connected.
> Check that the USB power supply provides power to something to another device, such as a cellular phone.
> Try a different power supply with your Raspberry Pi
> Check that the voltage of the supply is 5V and that a *minimum* of 750mA is being provided.

If the power light of the Raspberry Pi comes on, but there is no display please see 5.2.

5.2 Keyboard and Mouse Problems

If your mouse or keyboard is not recognised by the Raspberry Pi or operating system:

> Test the peripherals with another working computer if possible.
> Check the Internet to see if your model of keyboard or mouse is compatible with the Raspberry Pi

- ➤ Check the Internet to see if your model of keyboard or mouse is compatible with your chosen operating system.
- ➤ Make sure that the power draw of your peripherals does not exceed the design specifications of the Raspberry Pi. If they do, either substitute them with lower power replacements or use a powered USB hub.

5.3 Display Problems

If the power light of the Raspberry Pi comes on, but there is no display it is possible that the wrong display mode has been auto-selected. Try pressing one of the following keys on the keyboard to change display mode:

- ➤ **HDMI Mode,** which is the default. **Press 1**
- ➤ **HDMI safe mode,** if you're using an HDMI display and can't see anything, press 2.
- ➤ **Composite PAL mode** Press 3
- ➤ **Composite NTSC** Press 4

5.4 Problems with Booting

If your Raspberry Pi is not booting:

- ➤ Check that the power light is on.
- ➤ Follow the display troubleshooting tips under 5.3

➤ Check that the SD card is properly seated.
➤ Test the SD card in another computer
➤ Try booting the Raspberry Pi using a different Raspberry Pi SD card

5.5 Network Problems

If you are having a problem connecting to a wired or wireless network, check the following:

For Wired Networks:

➤ Do other computers connect successfully on the network?
➤ Does the Ethernet port link light come on?
➤ Does the Ethernet cable work with another computer?
➤ Is your router set for DHCP?

For Wireless Networks:

➤ Does the USB Wi-Fi work on other computers? If not replace it, if so then make sure it is compatible.
➤ Can other computers connect to the Wi-Fi network? If so re-check the settings in the Wi-Fi configuration tool. If not, refer to the router settings and manual.
➤ Has the router been set to broadcast the SSID (Network name)?

➢ Have you configured the Wi-Fi using the Raspbian Wi-Fi configuration tool?

Chapter 6: Where to From Here?

By following this guide you should be up and running with your Raspberry Pi, now it's time to begin exploring, learning and reaching the potential of the device. Perhaps you are interested in programming? You should look for a few of the wonderful guides to programming in Python (or any of the other supported languages) for the Raspberry Pi. Maybe you are interested in using the Raspberry Pi as a media streamer, a vintage arcade box, a control system for a home brewery or one of many other amazing projects. These and more can be found online.

Whatever it is that you decide to do with your Raspberry Pi, remember that this computer was designed to be played with. The worst that can happen is that you have to redo the SD card installation or perhaps replace the Raspberry Pi itself if there is a serious problem. This computer was designed for these scenarios; don't let these issues prevent you from learning from and enjoying the device. Good luck!

www.ingramcontent.com/pod-product-compliance
Lightning Source LLC
Chambersburg PA
CBHW060933050326
40689CB00013B/3077